MARKETPLACE PRAYERS

LOVING GOD, YOURSELF, AND OTHERS

CHRIS G. KERR

Marketplace Prayers: Loving God, Yourself, and Others

ISBN: 978-0-9880825-5-7

DEDICATION

I dedicate this book to my family and coworkers, both present and past. I honor my mother, my late father, my brothers and sisters, my nieces, nephews, their partners, one great niece, great nephews, my aunts, uncles, cousins, and those who will join us in the future, and those already in heaven. Prayer has transformed our family legacy for generations, and I am deeply grateful for the devoted prayers of our family members and ancestors. The legacy of "Marketplace Prayers" is meant to keep the flame of prayer alive for future generations. It aims to witness the salvation of family members, break generational cycles, and unlock blessings for those to come. I love you all.

A GIFT FOR YOU

BE A PART OF MARKETPLACE PRAYERS

God doesn't need everyone in the world praying and seeking Him to heal the land, He just needs His people to do it!

Calling all intercessors who want a positive transformation in their lives and know that intercessors need prayer, too.

I invite you to join the Marketplace Prayers Facebook group.

"For where two or three gather in my name, there am I with them." (Matthew 18:20)

Join the Facebook group at:
https://www.facebook.com/groups/marketplaceprayers

Visit the Website:

http://www.marketplaceprayers.com/

TABLE OF CONTENTS

INTRODUCTION

In the Bible, we are commanded and invited to experience love's transformative power. This love, when fully embraced, has the power to change our lives. We are called to love God, love ourselves, and love others. Jesus, in Matthew 22:37-39 NIV, beautifully articulates this: "Love the Lord your God with all your heart and with all our soul and with all your mind. This is the first and greatest commandment. And the second is like it: 'Love your neighbor as yourself.'" These commandments are not mere obligations but keys to unlocking a life filled with purpose, joy, and fulfillment. They are the seeds of transformation, waiting to be sown in your heart.

Many believers assume their love for God is automatic and overlook the importance of genuinely loving themselves and others. This journey of love requires intentionality, self-awareness, and a deep understanding of God's truth. It also involves recognizing the influence of spiritual forces. One such force is the enemy, often referred to as Satan or the Devil. He tries to deceive us with negative thoughts, making us believe they are our own. But remember, you have the power to discern and reject these lies, aligning your thoughts with God's truth. The Bible explains that Satan masquerades as an angel of light (2 Corinthians 11:14). He appears as one, but he is not the true light. He presents himself as a force for good rather than evil, but his true nature is revealed in the temptation of Jesus in the wilderness (Matthew 4:1-11). In this passage, Satan attempts to deceive Jesus by twisting Scripture and offering worldly power, yet Jesus resists him with the truth of God's Word. This should serve as a cautionary tale, reminding us to be vigilant against the deceptive nature of Satan.

Satan, the adversary, is not an angel of light but the father of lies (John 8:44). However, his defeat is not just a possibility, it is inevitable. Christ has triumphed over him, and Revelation 20:10 tells us that the day will come when the devil will be thrown into the lake of burning sulfur, to be tormented forever. Heaven is real, and so is hell. But remember, victory is assured. Which team are you on?

Each section of this book is designed to help you understand and embrace these vital aspects of love. You will find letters from the Heavenly Father and heartfelt prayers, providing you with the tools and insights you need for your journey.

SECTION ONE

LOVING GOD

CHAPTER ONE

FATHER, SON, AND HOLY SPIRIT

My Beloved Child,

From the dawn of creation, I, your Heavenly Father, have lovingly fashioned you with a unique purpose and a divine plan. Every detail of your being, I have carefully crafted with my own hands. I take immense delight in seeing you fulfill the destiny I have ordained for you. I know you intimately, down to the depths of your soul, and my desire for you is nothing but the best.

I am love, and there is no darkness or malice in me. As the perfect Father, I lavish you with everlasting love, seeking to build you up and improve your life. My heart overflows with affection for you, and I long to see you align your thoughts and beliefs with my truth.

My precious one: there are two types of identities-the false and the true. The false narrative is a product of deception, leading you to believe that you are someone you are not. It breeds discontentment and confusion, even going so far as to challenge the very essence of your being. But hear me clearly: I did not make mistakes when I formed you. You are fearfully and wonderfully made with a unique purpose ordained by me.

Beware, for the adversary, Satan, is the enemy who seeks to steal your identity and lead you astray. He whispers lies into your mind, masquerading as your own thoughts, with the sole intention of separating you from me, from others, and your true self. His schemes are subtle, his deceptions cunning, but I have equipped you with the discernment to see through his deceit. Stand firm in my love, knowing you are my workmanship, destined for greatness in my kingdom.

Do not be swayed by the enemy's ploys, for the scripture in Hosea 4:6 reminds you that destruction comes from a lack of knowledge of God's truth. Be anchored in my truth, for it sets you free from the snares of the evil one. My voice speaks through the noise, distractions, and chaos, offering guidance, wisdom, and love.

Love Father God

My Child,

Let me introduce myself to you. I am your loving Father who has loved you from the very start (Jeremiah 31:3). You have been my beloved since I created you in the womb (Psalm 139:13-14), and I was there when you entered this world (Isaiah 44:24). I am the One who formed you and placed you with the parents you have. It wasn't their choice, but Mine—I chose you first (Ephesians 1:4).

I created the world, and in the beginning I created the heavens and the earth. Now the earth was formless and empty, darkness was over the surface of the deep, and the Spirit of God was hovering over the waters. I said, let there be light, and there was light (Genesis 1:1-3). I am the way and the truth and the life (John 14:6). I have never left you nor forsaken you (Deuteronomy 31:6). I have been watching over you all along (Psalm 121:5-8). There have been some things that have been misaligned, but we are getting things realigned now (Romans 8:28). Once you invite me in, we can begin this journey together (Revelation 3:20).

With all My love, Your Heavenly Father

Invite Him into Your Heart and Life

Father God, I come to You today with a humble heart. I believe that Jesus Christ is Your Son, that He died on the cross for my sins, and that He rose from the dead.

I confess my sins to You and ask for Your forgiveness. I turn away from my old ways and invite Jesus to be the Lord and Savior of my life.

Please come into my heart and life, and help me to follow You and Your teachings every day. Fill me with Your Holy Spirit and guide me on this new path.

Thank You for Your grace, mercy, and love, in Jesus' name. Amen.

My Beloved,

If you said that prayer for the first time the angels and I are rejoicing in heaven right now and your name is now written in the Lamb's book of life. Let me share with you the beautiful mystery of the Holy Trinity. I am one God who exists in three distinct but equal persons: the Father, the Son, and the Holy Spirit.

As the Father, I am the creator and sustainer of the universe. Everything good that exists comes from me. I am all-powerful, all-knowing, and ever-present, your ultimate authority and loving parent.

My Son, Jesus Christ, is both fully divine and fully human. Through Him, I revealed myself to humanity. Jesus lived a sinless life on earth, performed miracles, taught about my kingdom, was crucified, and rose from the dead. His life and sacrifice are the way for you to be reconciled with me. Jesus is called the "Son of God" because of His unique relationship with me and His vital role in my plan for you.

The Holy Spirit is my presence active in the world today. The Holy Spirit guides, empowers, and comforts you, inspiring the scriptures, transforming your life, and helping you live according to my will.

To understand the Trinity, think of water: it can be liquid, ice, or steam, but it is always H_2O. Similarly, I am one being who exists in three persons. This is a profound mystery, but it shapes how you relate to me, emphasizing our relationship as a loving Father, a redeeming Son, and a guiding Spirit.

Embrace me with an open heart, and know that I am always with you, loving you and guiding you on this path.

It is important to be aware there is an enemy, Satan, who seeks to deceive and lead you astray. He is a counterfeit, a copycat who twists and distorts the truth.

Satan cannot create anything new. He only mimics and perverts what I have made. His goal is to confuse you, making it difficult to see the truth clearly. He disguises himself as an angel of light, pretending to be good and holy, but his intentions are to deceive and destroy.

Satan promotes a superficial faith, one that lacks depth and commitment. He manipulates your emotions, using fear, guilt, or the desire for acceptance to cloud your judgment and make his lies seem appealing.

To protect yourself from these deceptions, immerse yourself in my Word and seek the guidance of the Holy Spirit. Develop a deep and personal relationship with me, so you can discern truth from falsehood. Trust in my love and wisdom to guide you through the challenges and temptations you may face.

Remember, I am always with you, providing strength, wisdom, and protection. Stay close to me, and you will be able to recognize and resist the enemy's counterfeit ways.

With all My love and guidance,

Your Loving Creator

CHAPTER TWO

THE LOVE OF A HEAVENLY FATHER

Blessed Child,

Understanding the depth of my love for you and others is essential for your spiritual and emotional well-being. I call you to love your neighbors as yourself, but if you struggle with self-love, remember this truth: you can't fully extend love to others without first loving yourself. Love is my essence, and I call you to love others as I love you—unconditionally and forever.

Loving others and yourself can be challenging. Some people may seem unlovable, yet I call you to love them. You may feel unworthy of love, but I love you despite the flaws you may see. Love, joy, and acceptance are essential for you. I do not spread hatred or judgment but heal and restore you through my love and passion.

Your existence is intertwined with relationships—with me, others, and yourself. In John 15:12, I command you to love one another as I love you. But do you truly grasp the depth of my love?

My love surpasses all understanding, rooted in my eternal nature and boundless grace. It is unconditional, not based on actions or merits, but solely on my divine character. My love remains steadfast, providing comfort, strength, and guidance. I invite you into a relationship of trust and security where you are deeply cherished and infinitely valued.

Recognize that any thought that is not loving and kind comes from the enemy. Any spirit that is not of the Holy Spirit is not welcome. You have the power to resist its influence and embrace me. You can maintain a pure and focused mind by casting down vain imaginations and anything that exalts itself against my knowledge. Through prayer, study, and introspection, you can overcome this spirit and experience the transformative power in your life.

As you surrender, your heart will soften, allowing you to give and receive love freely. When you understand the depth of my love, your perspective will shift, and you will find peace in my unfailing presence.

Ultimately, love is a choice—to embrace faith and positivity. It's not infatuation or fleeting emotions but a steadfast commitment rooted in my love. As you abide in me, you become vessels of grace and compassion to those around you.

In every instance, consciously choose love over fear, kindness over bitterness, and compassion over resentment. For in love, you encounter my very essence. Love one another as I love you.

Everything I have belongs to you now. You, as an heir to me and a joint heir with Jesus, hold a position of utmost privilege. My fortunes are not a handout, but a testament to your esteemed status. You are an heir because you are my child. If you are a born-again believer in Christ Jesus, you are a child of God and an heir to all that belongs to me. You have full access to the largest inheritance known to man. As Romans 8:17 says, "Now if we are children, then we are heirs—heirs of God and co-heirs with Christ, if indeed we share in his sufferings in order that we may also share in his glory."

You are not just redeemed but free from the curse. Sickness, disease, poverty, lack, depression, and strife are all under the curse—they're not good and come from the enemy. I am good, and You are delivered from every single part of that curse. As Galatians 3:13 states, "Christ redeemed us from the curse of the law by becoming a curse for us, for it is written: 'Cursed is everyone who is hung on a pole.'" This liberation should fill you with hope and the assurance of a better future.

You are not just a sinner saved by grace; you are a joint heir with Jesus. You are raised to do my business for my kingdom. But remember, you can only begin to be effective in what I call you to once you see yourself the way I see you. This self-perception is a reflection and a source of empowerment and responsibility.

With endless love,

Your Heavenly Father

CHAPTER THREE

✝

ARE YOU MAD AT ME?

— • • ● • • —

Dear Beloved,

You may not realize it, but deep down, you feel anger toward me. It surfaces, especially when I say no to your requests. I understand your frustration; accepting a 'no' is hard when your heart is set on a 'yes.' Please trust that I always have your best interests at heart; sometimes, your desire is not what's best for you and is not part of my greater plan for your life.

It's perfectly okay to admit you're angry with me. I can handle it. I want to hear all about your frustrations. Please don't keep them bottled up inside. There's no need to implode with your feelings or explode with them—I want you to be open and share everything. Talk to me as if I am beside you because I am, always.

What is it that you're angry about? I know what's in your heart, but you must voice it to me. Is it about how things didn't turn out as you expected? Are you upset over a failed relationship, a career setback, an injury, or perhaps an experience of betrayal or disloyalty? It could be something else, like losing an opportunity, feeling overlooked, or personal failures that haunt you. I know you don't see everything behind the scenes—how I am orchestrating events for your ultimate good, protecting you from unknown dangers.

I am genuinely sorry for the pain you've endured. I see your physical, emotional, mental, and spiritual exhaustion. I know the trauma that has scarred you over the years, and I yearn to heal you completely. Will you let me?

Come to me with all your cares and concerns. You've been shouldering immense burdens, and I want to lift them from you. You may feel disconnected from me and the vibrant power of the Holy Spirit. Perhaps you're burnt out from past seasons or have fallen into condemnation, resentment, or compromise. I am sorry you've felt the weight of the enemy's attacks.

But today, I call you to rise again. I have called you to be a warrior, and I am here to strengthen you so you will fight back. Together, we are better. You are not alone in this. A brand new day is dawning for you, a day of revival that starts with you. I will pour my resurrection life into you so you will rise to fulfill the true plan and purpose I have for you.

Are you ready to forgive me, to release your hurt, and to embrace the newness I offer? I am here, waiting with open arms. Be all wrapped up in the Lord.

With unending love,

Your Master Healer

Are you ready to forgive? Write your forgiveness prayer to me here.

_____

_____

_____

_____

This short list of characteristics highlights the different aspects of my nature and is foundational to understanding my identity according to my Word in the Bible.

1. Omnipotent (All-powerful) - Revelation 19:6
2. Omniscient (All-knowing) - Psalm 147:5
3. Omnipresent (Everywhere) - Psalm 139:7-10
4. Eternal - Deuteronomy 33:27
5. Immutable (Unchanging) - Malachi 3:6
6. Holy - Isaiah 6:3
7. Just - Deuteronomy 32:4
8. Loving - 1 John 4:8
9. Merciful - Ephesians 2:4-5
10. Faithful - 2 Timothy 2:13
11. Sovereign - Daniel 4:35
12. Good - Psalm 34:8
13. Gracious - Psalm 103:8
14. Wise - Romans 11:33
15. Self-existent - Exodus 3:14
16. Self-sufficient - John 5:26
17. Righteous - Psalm 11:7
18. Infinite - Jeremiah 23:24
19. Transcendent - Isaiah 55:8-9
20. Personal - John 10:14-15
21. Compassionate - Psalm 103:13
22. Forgiving - 1 John 1:9
23. Creator - Genesis 1:1
24. Sustainer - Colossians 1:17
25. Healer - Exodus 15:26
26. Redeemer - Isaiah 44:22
27. Shepherd - Psalm 23:1
28. Light - 1 John 1:5

Let's Pray:

Father God, please forgive me for not believing that You have my best interests at heart. Why is it that whenever I say I don't want something to happen a certain way, that is how it happens. I feel like You aren't listening to me. I know You are God, and I'm not, but when will I see better things in my life? When will the desires of my heart come to fruition? I know an enemy exists, and I am sick of him. Get him out of my life. Is what I'm dealing with what spiritual warfare looks like? Is this You? Is this part of my training, or am I just making bad decisions? Why do cycles of the same struggles keep coming up?

Lord, I acknowledge my calling to love and assist others, and I confess that I sometimes struggle with this task. It can be overwhelming, and I often find myself in need of Your guidance. I ask for Your wisdom and patience to navigate these challenging interactions, and I understand that I have a role to play in this process.

Lord, I need Your strength and wisdom to face these challenges. I ask for Your help in trusting Your plan and timing, even when it is beyond my comprehension. Show me how to break free from these recurring cycles and make decisions that align with Your will. Help me to love others as You have called me to, even when it is difficult. I surrender my frustrations and doubts to You, knowing that You are always there to guide me. If this is of my own accord, please bring alignment back to my life. Lead me, Lord, and renew my faith in Your goodness and love in Jesus' name. Amen!

My Dear Child,

There is a battle within you, my dear one. Thoughts that are not always from Me, but from the enemy or your flesh may arise. Yet, you have the power to align these thoughts with My Word. Take every thought captive to make it obedient to Christ (2 Corinthians 10:5). I long to see you healed and delivered. To be free from mental torment, you must choose to walk in My truth every day.

With the multitude of thoughts that flood your mind daily, it's natural to feel overwhelmed. But remember, thoughts become words, words become actions, and actions become behaviors. Your thoughts shape who you are. Do not let negative thoughts linger. While you may not be able to control every thought that enters your mind, you have the power to reject the negative ones the enemy brings. Guard your heart, for everything you do flows from it (Proverbs 4:23). Don't let your spring be poisoned, for whoever drinks the water I give them will never thirst. Indeed, the water I give them will become in them a spring of water welling up to eternal life (John 4:14).

Reflect on the fruit you are producing. Are you coming closer to Me or moving further away? By abiding in Me, you will bear much fruit; apart from Me, you can do nothing (John 15:5). Remember, hatred stirs up conflict, but love covers over all wrongs (Proverbs 10:12).

Like Job, who said, "What I feared has come upon me; what I dreaded has happened to me. I have no peace, no quietness; I have no rest, but only turmoil" (Job 3:25-26), you may feel overwhelmed by fear and unrest. But I am with you always, guiding you.

Remember to renew your mind daily with My Word (Romans 12:2). "Then you will know the truth, and the truth will set you free." (John 8:32)

With endless love,

Your Heavenly Father

SECTION TWO

LOVING YOURSELF

CHAPTER FOUR

I LOVE YOU

My Faithful One,

I love you unconditionally, to the very core of your being. Why are you so harsh with yourself? If anyone else treated a friend as you treat yourself, you would not stand for it. Why not allow yourself the grace of a break? Why push yourself so relentlessly? I already love you—you don't have to earn my love through constant striving. You can be... just be yourself. Remember, "I have loved you with an everlasting love; I have drawn you with unfailing kindness" (Jeremiah 31:3).

You were made perfect in your uniqueness because you are created in my image (Genesis 1:27). Yet, you are so hard on yourself. Who told you that you were a mistake? Who has been deceiving you? The enemy is a liar, and you must reject those negative thoughts he plants in your mind. It's time to stop agreeing with the lies you've been told. It is finished. Let that mindset end now.

It would help if you stopped berating yourself over every little thing. Remember, "The tongue has the power of life and death" (Proverbs 18:21), and sadly, your words have not been bringing you life. I see your struggles and your inability to forgive yourself but know this: nothing you have done can separate you from my love (Romans 8:38-39). My love for you is unconditional.

It's time for you to embrace self-forgiveness. You have been burdened with guilt, shame, and condemnation—emotions and weights that you were never meant to bear. Please hand them over to me. I want you to see your worth, your beauty, and your value as I see you. You are one-of-a-kind and exquisitely unique.

Let go of body shaming. I created your body, and I made no mistakes. "You are fearfully and wonderfully made." Let's begin the healing from the inside so it can manifest outwardly. Let my love begin this transformation within you.

I desire you to love as I love: love me, yourself, and others. This is the essence of my commandment, "Love your neighbor as yourself" (Mark 12:31). You have tried so hard to be perfect, to meet every expectation, but I know that striving is exhausting. I want you to be at peace with yourself. There is nothing wrong with you.

Reject the enemy's voice that keeps you trapped in a cycle of self-criticism. I am putting an end to that now. Today is new, and you will embrace who you were meant to be. Give yourself a break and treat yourself with kindness. Are you ready to forgive yourself?

With infinite love,

Your Heavenly Father

Are you ready to forgive? Write your forgiveness prayer to me here.

_____

_____

_____

_____

Let's Pray:

Heavenly Father,

I humbly ask for Your forgiveness for the times I've failed to love myself as You love me. I confess that I believed the lies of the enemy and the hurtful words spoken about me. I repent for the times I've fallen short of walking in love and for any instance of rejecting others. I acknowledge my rebelliousness and my distance from Your perfect love.

Lord, I am in awe of Your unconditional love that surpasses all understanding. I am grateful that You loved me first and enabled me to love another. I am thankful that Your love for me is not based on anything I do but simply because of who You are. Your love is boundless, and nothing can separate me from it.

Thank You, Father, for the capacity to receive love from others freely. Help me to embrace Your love fully and to extend it to those around me.

Lord, I acknowledge that You knew me even before You formed me in the womb. You have set me apart and ordained my life's path. I am grateful for Your divine plan for my existence.

I choose to walk in Your image, loving You, myself, and others as You love. I wholeheartedly accept myself just as I am and commit to loving others unconditionally. I declare that I am a new creation, redeemed and covered by the blood of Jesus Christ. I am grateful for Your unfailing goodness and faithfulness.

I rejoice that I am Your child, destined for greatness. I reject every lie and accusation hurled against me, knowing I am Your heir and made in Your image.

Thank You, Lord, for the freedom You have granted me. I declare Your truth over my life—I am loved, lovable, accepted, secure, confident, and cared for in the name of Jesus. Amen.

My dear child,

When you confess your sins, I will forgive and cleanse you from all unrighteousness. There is no record of your past mistakes; the blood of Jesus washes them away. You are made new in my eyes.

Do not carry the burden of guilt or shame. Come to me freely, knowing that my mercy is boundless and my love for you is everlasting. Each day is a fresh start, a new opportunity to walk in my grace and love.

Remember, my child, that my forgiveness is not conditional. It is a gift given freely because of my deep love for you. Embrace this truth and live in the freedom it brings.

With all My love,

Your Faithful Father

MARKETPLACE PRAYERS

CHAPTER FIVE

WHO DO YOU SAY I AM?

—— · · • · · ——

My love,

You were intricately designed with a purpose, woven together in the womb with care and intentionality. I know your innermost desires and dreams, and I am guiding you towards a path that leads to greater fulfillment and joy. As your Father, I affectionately call you my beloved child, longing to nurture and transform your life for the better.

In my love, there is no malice or cruelty—only the purity and goodness embodying my nature. I extend my boundless love to you with unwavering devotion, as the epitome of what a perfect father's love should be. My love for you is unfailing and eternal, a love that surpasses all understanding and is always there, lifting you up and strengthening you (Ephesians 3:18-19).

As you immerse yourself in the eternal truth of my Word, your mind will be renewed and your heart softened. Through this transformation, healing begins to take root, bringing profound change to every aspect of your life. This renewal is not just a momentary change but a lasting shift that aligns your thoughts with my will, allowing you to walk in freedom and truth.

Let us rejoice in the affirmations I provide, embracing my unwavering love that seeks to reveal the depth of my affection for you. I desire to be your guide and your comforter and stronghold in times of need. Trust in my perfect timing and plan for your life, for I am always at work in you, accomplishing what will bring the most glory to my name and the greatest joy to your life (Philippians 2:13).

My presence goes with you, providing peace that defies understanding and joy that is complete. Lean on me, rely on my strength, and find peace in my love. You are my beloved, and in you, I find great delight.

With all My love,

Your Father God

Let's Pray:

Heavenly Father, I come to You seeking Your gentle intervention. Please quiet the voices of deception and confusion that seek to mislead me. Let Your loving hand purify the airwaves of all communication channels, dispelling any enemy's influence, in the mighty name of Jesus—a name that reigns above all.

Father, I ask Your ministering angels to gently remove any obstacles and darkness hindering Your work in my life. Grant me a deep peace that fills my mind, body, and spirit, wrapping me in the comfort of

Your love as I find security in my identity in Christ. I am grateful for the strength of Your protection and the confidence it instills in me.

I renounce all false identities, lies, and deceitful schemes set against me. By the authority You have given me through Jesus Christ, I break free from the chains of falsehood and distortion. I declare that You make every crooked path straight, and I dismiss every spirit of confusion, delusion, disruption, and disorder in Jesus' mighty name.

Lord, replace negativity within me with Your liberating truth, drawing us closer and guiding our lives. Fill me abundantly with the assurance of who I am in Christ, whom You created me to be, and the true purpose You have ordained for my life. May Your truth resonate within me, fostering confidence, restoration, wholeness, and completeness in Jesus' name. Amen.

My Dearest Child,

I want you to hear this from me, your loving Father:

- ✓ You are deeply cherished by me, explicitly chosen as my own. My love for you is profound and unending.

- ✓ You are my child, forgiven and redeemed through the precious blood of Jesus. "You are forever cleansed and eternally mine.

- ✓ You stand secure in your identity in Christ, liberated from all deceit and confinement. Embrace the freedom I have given you, free from all that once held you bound.

- ✓ My peace, which surpasses all understanding, fills your heart and guards your mind. Let this peace be your shield and comfort.

- ✓ Empowered by the Holy Spirit, you walk in truth and exhibit the virtues of your Savior. These traits are the evidence of my

Spirit within you.

- ✓ You are valued and loved beyond measure, accepted and beloved in my sight. You are fully equipped to fulfill the unique purpose I have planned for you. I have prepared you for great things.

- ✓ Angelic beings surround you, ministering and protecting you from the adversary's assaults. You are never alone. My heavenly hosts guard and guide you.

Remember, you are known and seen by me, the Creator of the universe. In my eyes, you are perfect, crafted with purpose and intention. Embrace who you are, knowing you stand on the solid ground of my truth. Your life is a testament to my design, filled with sincerity and clarity. You are trustworthy, righteous, and direct, steered by my wisdom. Walk confidently in your divine purpose, embracing the fullness of who you are meant to be.

With all My everlasting love,

Your Chief Cornerstone

CHAPTER SIX

YOUR IDENTITY

My Chosen Child,

Empower yourself to take command of your thoughts and focus on embracing the truth I have spoken about your identity. It is crucial to reject the enemy's lies that lead to destruction and illness. Understand that your thoughts shape your future and influence your destiny. Negative thought patterns and words significantly contribute to sickness and disease.

While it may be challenging to shift your mindset, actively redirect your thoughts towards the truths found in My Word. By identifying and rejecting the lies, you can replace them with the promises I have made to you in the scriptures. This will renew your mind and reveal your true identity in me.

Meditating on my Word is essential for transforming your life. When you immerse yourself in Scripture, you open your heart and mind to receive my divine wisdom, truth, and guidance. Through meditation, you allow the Holy Spirit to illuminate the words, bringing understanding, insight, and revelation.

In the garden of truth, I have planted for you, love, joy, peace, patience, kindness, goodness, faithfulness, gentleness, self-control, health, wisdom, knowledge, and integrity flourish abundantly. These are the fruits of a life lived in my Spirit and yours to claim.

However, nearby looms a stark contrast—a formidable fortress of strongholds seeking to entrap us. This wall includes rejection, shame, guilt, criticism, judgment, anger, revenge, hate, abandonment, unforgiveness, anxiety, fear, intimidation, control, isolation, withdrawal, rebellion, pride, victimhood, worry, depression, grief, lies, death, manipulation, procrastination, hopelessness, accusations, defeat, infirmity, addictions, and self-hate.

Do not dwell in the shadows of these strongholds. Instead, step into the light of my garden of truth, where you will find refuge—a place of discernment, understanding, fearlessness, victory, overcoming, bravery, honesty, caring, hopefulness, trustworthiness, obedience, freedom from debt, and honor.

I have laid before you the path of life; choose to walk in it, and let my Word be a lamp to your feet and a light to your path (Psalm 119:105). Embrace the fullness of life I offer you, and let my truths shape your thoughts and actions.

As you meditate on my Word, your thoughts will align with my truth, replacing negative, worldly thinking with my perspective. This renewal process is transformative, reshaping your attitudes, beliefs, and behaviors to reflect the character of Christ.

Meditating on my Word strengthens your relationship with me, deepens your faith, and empowers you to live according to my will. Remember, you were authentically made in Christ. You were born beautifully and wonderfully made to fulfill the purpose I have for you.

Embrace this journey of transformation and let my Word guide you every step of the way.

Here are some truths about who you are in me, deeply rooted in my Word:

1. You can do all things through Christ who gives you strength. (Philippians 4:13)

2. You are a child of God. (Romans 8:14-16)

3. Through faith, you are saved by grace. (Ephesians 2:8)

4. You will always praise me. (Psalms 34:1)

5. You are a disciple and follower of Jesus. (Matthew 5:1-2)

6. You are the righteousness of God. (2 Corinthians 5:21)

7. You are my co-worker. (1 Corinthians 3:9)

8. You fix your eyes on what is unseen, not on what is seen. (2 Corinthians 4:18)

9. You do not conform to this world but are transformed by the renewing of your mind. (Romans 12:1-2)

10. You take captive every thought to make it obedient to Christ. (2 Corinthians 10:5)

11. You live by faith, not by sight. (2 Corinthians 5:7)

12. You are an overcomer. (1 John 4:4)

13. You are the head and not the tail, at the top and not the bottom. (Deuteronomy 28:13)

14. You have authority to trample over the power of the enemy. (Luke 10:19)

15. By His wounds, you are healed. (1 Peter 2:24)

16. You are blessed with every spiritual blessing in Christ. (Ephesians 1:3)

17. You have eternal life through the Son of God. (1 John 5:11-12)

18. You are blessed when you come in and blessed when you go out. (Deuteronomy 28:6)

19. Your work is blessed by the Lord. (Deuteronomy 28:12)

20. You are an heir of God and a co-heir with Christ. (Romans 8:17)

21. You are strong in the Lord and in His mighty power. (Ephesians 6:10)

22. You cast all your cares on me, for I care for you deeply. (1 Peter 5:7)

23. All of your needs are met by Jesus. (Philippians 4:19)

24. You are guarded by my angels wherever you go. (Psalm 91:11-12)

25. You participate in my divine nature. (2 Peter 1:4)

26. You are a new creation in Christ. (2 Corinthians 5:17)

27. You are sanctified and justified. (1 Corinthians 6:11)

28. You have peace with God through Christ. (Romans 5:1)

29. I redeem you from the enemy. (Psalm 107:2)

30. You are a chosen person, a royal priesthood, a holy nation, my special possession. (1 Peter 2:9)

31. You are chosen by me. (Romans 8:33)

32. You are redeemed and forgiven through His blood. (Ephesians 1:7)

33. You are submitted to God; when you resist the devil, he flees from you. (James 4:7)

34. You were given a spirit not of fear but of power, love, and discipline. (2 Timothy 1:7)

Embrace these truths, my child, for in them brings the freedom and identity I have placed upon you. You are so dearly loved and highly favored in my eyes. Stand firm in this identity and live out the calling I have placed upon your life with confidence and joy.

With boundless love,

Your Abba Father

CHAPTER SEVEN

I LOVE YOUR NEIGHBORS

My Beloved Child,

I have spoken to you about this before, and it is worth repeating: love your neighbor as yourself. This foundational commandment reflects my love and is a pathway to a harmonious and fulfilling life. It means treating others with the same kindness, respect, and care that you desire for yourself. This simple yet profound principle can transform your relationships and bring peace to your community.

Forgive them for every time they were noisy; for those moments, they were unmannerly or failed to take care of their yard. Forgive them when they park in your space, play too loud music, let their pets roam freely, or for being nosy and talking about you. Forgive them for misunderstandings, harsh words, or any actions that caused you inconvenience or discomfort. Remember, forgiveness is not a sign of weakness, but a source of strength. As I have forgiven you, extend that same grace to your neighbors, knowing that it has the power to transform relationships and bring peace.

Remember what is written in Psalm 62:4-6:

"Surely they intend to topple me
from my lofty place;
they take delight in lies.
With their mouths they bless,
but in their hearts they curse

Yes, my soul, find rest in God;
my hope comes from him.
Truly he is my rock and my salvation;
he is my fortress, I will not be shaken."

From My perspective, these verses remind you that even when others' intentions may seem negative or their actions unsettling, your peace and hope come from Me. I am your rock and your fortress. I am unshakeable. When you rest in Me, you are secure and can extend forgiveness and love to others, regardless of their behavior.

Bless your neighbors on purpose with your thoughts. Instead of harboring resentment or frustration, choose to pray for their well-being. Ask for My blessings upon their lives, families, and homes. Pray for their health, their relationships, their work, and their spiritual journey. When you bless others in this way, you open the door for My grace to flow more abundantly in your life and theirs.

Loving your neighbor as yourself is not always easy, but it is always powerful. It is a testament to My love working through you, a tangible expression of the love I have for each of you. As you forgive and bless, you will find greater peace and fulfillment in your life. My grace is sufficient for you, and My strength is perfect in your weakness.

Rest in My love, and let it overflow to your neighbors. In doing so, you will be living out My commandment and experiencing the fullness of life I have promised.

With all My love,

Your Heavenly Father

SECTION THREE
LOVING FAMILY

CHAPTER EIGHT

I LOVE YOUR PARENTS

—— · · ● · · ——

I love Your Dad

My Precious Gem, I understand that you may project your experiences with your earthly Father onto me, your Heavenly Father. This is a tool of the enemy, fostering a false image of me as distant or mean. But this portrayal is far from the truth.

I saw what happened with your earthly Father. I saw how he hurt you, and my heart ached for you. I cried with you, for I never meant for you to be broken. Your earthly Father had a choice to make, and sadly, he chose the wrong one. He did not know any better, and his actions did not reflect my love for you. I am sorry that he wasn't there for you as I intended a parent to be.

I am profoundly sorry for the pain you endured. On behalf of your Dad, I humbly ask for your forgiveness. I never intended for you to experience such hurt. Please find it in your heart to forgive me. Please find it in your heart to forgive him.

I am steadfast in your life, ready to embrace you with open arms and heal your wounds. My love for you is not characterized by cruelty or tyranny but by boundless love and compassion. I will never abandon you; my love for you is unwavering and unconditional, like that of a nurturing and caring parent.

Are you ready to forgive? Your forgiveness is a powerful act of love and healing. Write your forgiveness prayer to me here:

_____

_____

_____

_____

Please note: Forgiveness is a continuous process, not a single prayer. Even if you believe you have forgiven someone, be prepared to forgive again as feelings and memories resurface.

I Love Your Mom

I want to speak to you about your mother and the journey she has been through.

I am deeply sorry for what your mom had to go through. The challenges she faced, the wounds she carried, and the battles she fought were not easy. I am sorry that she wasn't always emotionally available for you and couldn't provide the support and nurturing you needed. She did her best with what she had, but I know it wasn't always enough.

Your mother, despite her struggles, loves you very much. This may be hard to hear and believe, but it is true. Your Mom and Dad love you deeply, even if they can't always show it in the ways you need. They have always been proud of you, watching your growth and achievements with a love that may not have always been expressed but has always been there.

They have always been for you, not against you, even though it may have sometimes felt different. Their own limitations and difficulties sometimes made it hard for them to express their love and pride clearly. But know this: you are so loved by them. You are their sweet baby, and you will always be their baby, regardless of age.

You are deeply cherished not only by your earthly parents but also by me, your Heavenly Father. My love for you is perfect and unwavering. I see your pain, your struggles, and your triumphs. I celebrate you in every moment.

I am here to fill the gaps, to heal the wounds, and to provide the love and support that may have been lacking. Your parents, in their imperfect way, tried to love you the best they could. And I, your perfect Father, am here to surround you with my boundless love and grace.

You are precious to me, and I will always be with you, guiding, comforting, and loving you with everlasting love.

Are you ready to forgive? Write your forgiveness prayer to me here:

_____

_____

_____

_____

Dear Cherished One, thank you for coming to me and seeking forgiveness. Seeing your heart open and ready for healing brings me great joy. The next step is to bless and honor those you need to forgive. This act of blessing will bring true freedom and peace to your heart.

When you speak blessings over others, you align your heart with mine. Even if you don't know what to say, simply saying "I bless them, I bless them, I bless them" is powerful. Your words have the power to bring life and transformation.

Pray favor over them. Ask for strength and energy for their daily lives. Pray that they will live happily all their lives and that their youth will be renewed like the eagles. Cover them with a shield of love, honor, and compassion.

Pray for peace, abundance, and success in their lives. Ask for my favor to be with them, guiding and protecting them in all they do. When you pray these blessings, you are not only helping them but also healing your own heart.

Pray Psalm 91 over them, asking for divine protection and the assurance that they will dwell in the shelter of the Most High, under my wings, safe and secure.

As you bless and honor them, you reflect my love and grace. You become a vessel of my peace and a beacon of my light. This practice will deepen your relationship with me and strengthen your spirit.

Remember, I am always with you, guiding and supporting you in every step you take. Lean on me, trust in my love, and continue to walk in my grace.

Love always,

Abba Father

Let's Honor YOUR Mother and Father

Heavenly Father, I come to Your throne of grace with a heart full of gratitude to honor and bless my mother and Father, as well as all the caring people who have been an influence in my life. I bless them for everything they have done for me, for their love, support, and guidance. I thank You that they are a positive influence on me. Their wisdom, patience, and love have shaped who I am, and I want to acknowledge them today.

You have ordained and selected me to be part of this family, and I am deeply grateful for that. I cherish and love them dearly. They are dear to my heart, and I appreciate them more than words express. I pray that You will bless them abundantly. Shower them with Your grace, and fill their lives with peace, joy, and happiness all the days of their lives.

I pray for Your divine protection over them. Guard them in all their ways and keep them safe from harm. May they feel encouraged and respected, knowing they are valued and loved. I ask for a shield of favor around them everywhere they go. Let Your favor be upon them, opening doors of opportunity and blessing them in every aspect of their lives.

Grant them strength and good health, and may they continue to be a source of inspiration and love to those around them. Pour out Your blessings upon them, providing for all their needs and granting the desires of their hearts.

Thank You for Your loving kindness and faithfulness. I trust in Your promises and know that You will continue to watch over them and bless them richly in Jesus' mighty name. Amen.

CHAPTER NINE

✝

I LOVE YOUR SIBLINGS

———— ·•●•· ————

Dear Child,

I know your brothers and sisters and their children—and even their children's children, who are yet to be born. I have already crafted a plan for them so that your whole family will know me and love me as you do. I see your care for their well-being and your faithful prayers. Life presents its challenges, and everyone has choices to make.

I understand your longing to be closer to your siblings and your desire for their best, just as they wish the best for you. I am aware of what each of your brothers and sisters is experiencing. My will is for them to draw nearer to me, but the choice is theirs. I never force them; instead, I gently nudge them, always trying to catch their attention.

I see the depths of your heart and how earnestly you want them to choose me. I am deeply grateful when you stand in the gap and pray for them. Know that I hear every prayer and collect every tear. You can confide in me about anything that troubles you regarding your family.

What burdens are you carrying about them? Are you ready to forgive and release every burden to me? I am here, listening, and ready to lighten your load as you trust in my perfect timing and plan for you and your loved ones. Let us walk this path together, hand in hand, as you lay down your worries and embrace my peace.

In My everlasting love,

Your Sovereign Lord

Are you ready to forgive? Write your forgiveness prayer to me here.

_____

_____

_____

_____

Please note: Forgiveness is a continuous process, not a single prayer. Even if you believe you have forgiven someone, be prepared to forgive again as feelings and memories resurface.

CHAPTER TEN

✝

I LOVE YOUR CHILD

— • • ● • • —

If you, like me, haven't given birth to a child, this chapter might prompt you to reflect on the children currently in your life or your desire to have children. You will also find a letter from God revealing His heart to break off barrenness.

Dear Beloved,

I cherish your children deeply. In my Word, I have said, "Let the little children come to me, and do not hinder them, for the kingdom of heaven belongs to such as these" (Matthew 19:14). This scripture reminds us to embrace a child-like faith and innocence, qualities I adore in your children.

I see all that you have done to raise them. Under the circumstances, you've performed admirably. While I may not have provided a manual for raising children, know that it truly does take a village, and you've done well with the support you had. I am proud of you and grateful for your dedication, sacrifice, and the countless sleepless nights you endured in pursuing raising them.

Parenting is a full-time job requiring a supernatural strength I have placed upon you. Whenever you feel tired or overwhelmed, come and sit with me. Let me refill your cup; you cannot run on empty. I am here to restore your strength and energy. Even if it's only five minutes, rest with me. I will fill you with peace and renew your ability to continue during this time.

Remember, I love your children deeply, and each name holds a significant meaning. I have plans for them, plans to prosper them and not to harm them, to give them hope and a future, as affirmed in Jeremiah 29:11.

I understand the pain you've felt due to their actions and how they've treated you. While their behavior may have been hurtful, I ask you to forgive. In doing so, I will heal your heart and mend the wounds caused by their actions.

Please know that my love for you and them is unending. Lean on me, and let my love and strength be your guide and comfort as you continue this journey of parenthood.

With endless love,

Your Almighty God

Are you ready to forgive? Write your forgiveness prayer to me here.

_____

_____

_____

_____

Breaking Free from Barrenness

My Beloved Child,

My Word, as written in Psalm 127:3, declares, "Children are a heritage from the Lord, offspring a reward from him." This divine blessing, this sacred heritage, is not to be taken lightly. I am aware of the many families seeking this blessing and heritage from me. I want you to know that I am extending my supernatural grace and healing to all, including the womb in need of my touch. I am here to restore health and align each one, granting childless couples the precious gift of a family. I will remove all barrenness and break every chain that hinders this blessing in Jesus' name.

I see the hearts of those who long for children yet have faced disappointment and heartache. I am wrapping my comforting arms around them, renewing their strength and faith. Remember my promises, and let your hearts be filled with hope and peace that surpasses all understanding.

I am thankful for the fruitful and multiplying families fulfilling their divine purpose, which is to love and nurture the children I have blessed them with. I rejoice in the joy and laughter children bring into your lives. May these families continue to grow in love, health, and unity. Let your homes be filled with my presence and peace, nurturing each member to thrive in my purpose.

I also see those who have been divinely called to adopt or foster children. I bless this sacred mission with the resources, support, and love they need to open their hearts and homes. May they experience the profound joy and fulfillment of raising children in my love and truth.

I am grateful for new births, health, hope, and joy. My blessings will continue to flow abundantly, aligning with your assignment. Let every child born into these families testify to my faithfulness and goodness. I will raise them to be strong, healthy, and full of My Spirit, equipped to fulfill my plans for their lives.

With everlasting love,

Father God

CHAPTER ELEVEN

✝

I LOVE YOUR GRANDPARENTS

• • ● • • ——

My Treasured One,

I see the depths of your heart and the feelings you carry toward your grandparents, great-grandparents, and all those who came before you. I know you sometimes feel overlooked, as if others are favored over you. Yet, I assure you, their love for you is deep and genuine, as if you were their very own.

If you have any hurt feelings or unresolved pain regarding your grandparents or great-grandparents, I encourage you to lay these burdens down at my feet. There are many dynamics and stories in your family history that you may not be aware of—struggles, sacrifices, and decisions made in different times and contexts. I am fully aware of these intricacies and here to bring healing and clarity.

I call you to forgive. Forgive your grandparents for any hurt or misunderstandings. Forgive your ancestors and extend this grace through your family line to Adam. This act of forgiveness is powerful; it frees you from carrying the weight of past generations and opens the door to new blessings.

I want to cleanse and heal your family line, removing obstacles that have hindered blessings from flowing freely. As you release these grievances and choose forgiveness, you allow my love and mercy to work through your lineage, healing past wounds and bringing to light the generational blessings I have in store for you.

Remember, my child, that you are a crucial link in this chain of generations. Your decisions, forgiveness, and love can transform not just your life but the lives of those who come after you. I am with you in this journey, guiding, loving, and blessing you abundantly.

Stand firm in my promises and watch as I work through your acts of forgiveness to bring healing and restoration to your family. You are my cherished child, and I delight in setting things right for you and your lineage.

With unending love and infinite grace,

Your Great I Am

Are you ready to forgive? Write your forgiveness prayer to me here.

_____

_____

_____

_____

CHAPTER TWELVE

I LOVE YOUR NIECES AND NEPHEWS

My Sweet Baby, I want you to know how deeply I love your nieces, nephews, great-nieces, and great-nephews. I cherish each of them, understanding their hearts and the paths they have yet to walk. Yes, I am aware of those who are still to come into your family, and my hand is upon them as well.

I understand that sometimes disappointment can cloud your judgment, but remember, I am at work in their lives, teaching and guiding them so they can reach their highest potential. Thank you for your steadfast prayers over the years; they have made a significant impact. You might have noticed changes in their behaviors and mindsets—this transformation is part of my work in their hearts.

Continue to love them unconditionally. I know there have been times when they weren't kind to you or hurt you without intending to. Understand that they have faced their struggles and sometimes do not know how to express their feelings appropriately. Though not always loving or friendly, their actions were manifestations of their inner turmoil and not a reflection of their feelings toward you.

I am always watching over them, guiding them gently towards my love. Please continue to pray for them so they might come to know my love profoundly and choose to follow me. They genuinely are good children, and I have great plans for them. Pray that they make wise choices and remain under my protection.

I encourage you to keep praying Psalm 91 over them, claiming my promises of safety and refuge for their lives. Forgive them for past grievances, release any hurt, and let your words be filled with life and blessings whenever you pray or speak about them. Your words can uplift and transform, reflecting the love and appreciation you have for them and my love for them, too.

Speak to and about them with kindness and affirmation, for everyone yearns to be loved and appreciated. Know that I am watching over them and protecting them at every turn.

Remember to pray for their children and the generations yet unborn. They are the bearers of the future, and your prayers lay a foundation of faith and grace that will guide them throughout their lives.

You are a beacon of my love in their lives, and through your prayers and love, you can help them understand my deep love for them. Thank you for being such a faithful vessel of my love.

With all My love and blessings,

Your Faithful Redeemer

Are you ready to forgive? Write your forgiveness prayer to me here.

_____

_____

_____

_____

CHAPTER THIRTEEN

I LOVE ALL OF YOUR FAMILY

My Dear Child,

I want to assure you that I have remembered all your family members. I hold your aunts, uncles, cousins, in-laws, step-family, half-family, bonus family members, their spouses, and all extended relatives, near and far, in my loving embrace.

I urge you not to worry, for worry distracts from the trust you are called to place in Me. Remember, worry is a burden you were never meant to carry, and trusting in me frees you from its weight. Continue to pray fervently for unity within your family. I understand that some family members have not seen each other for years; such separations can heal, often more quickly than you might expect, when individuals choose forgiveness over resentment.

Unforgiveness can indeed implant bitterness within the heart, hindering healing and unity. Keep praying for softened hearts among your relatives, that they might relinquish their grievances and allow me to take My rightful place in their lives. Many need to let go of their desire for control and the need always to be correct—these are but trivial matters in the grand scheme of life.

Life is too short for such burdens, and I am here, waiting to bring healing and peace to your family. Do not cease in your prayers for them. Hold onto my promises, for I have assured you that your household will be saved. Remind me of my words, cling to my promises, and watch the transformation within your family unfold.

Now, I ask you, are you ready to forgive? Forgiveness is the key to the healing and unity I desire for you and your loved ones. It is a powerful act that can change the course of your family's history, bringing about a legacy of love and peace.

Stay steadfast in your faith and persistent in your prayers. Your trust in me nurtures the ground for miracles and blessings. I am faithful, and my plans for you and your family are for prosperity and hope.

With unending love and infinite compassion,

Your Prince of Peace

Are you ready to forgive? Write your forgiveness prayer to me here.

_____

_____

_____

_____

CHAPTER FOURTEEN

✝

I LOVE YOUR PETS

— • • ● • • —

My Loving Child,

I created animals as a special gift just for you, to fill your life with joy, companionship, and unconditional love. These precious creatures reflect my tender care and creativity, designed to enrich your days with their playful spirits and unwavering loyalty. In their eyes, you can see glimpses of My pure love; in their presence, you can find comfort and happiness, a soothing balm for life's trials. Whether it's the wagging tail of a dog greeting you at the door, the soothing purr of a cat on your lap, or the gentle nuzzle of your faithful furbaby friend, know that pets are my way of showing you how deeply I care for you and want you to experience love and joy through all My creations.

I am so sorry when you lost your pet. I know how much they meant to you and how heartbroken you were when they passed away. Even though you didn't see me, I was there to comfort you. I cared deeply about the pain you endured because I care about you and your beloved pet. I see how long you have grieved for your furbaby, and my heart aches with yours.

I understand that even your pets are loved like family members. I am deeply sorry for your loss, and I see the grief and heartache you endured.

Your pet brought joy, companionship, and unconditional love into your life. I placed them with you for a reason, knowing the bond you would share. Pets are a special gift, but they are not meant for every season of your life. While their time with you may have been shorter than you hoped, the love you shared was profound and meaningful.

I understand that you may not fully grasp why this loss happened, but I ask you to forgive and trust in my greater plan. Allow me to heal your heart completely and remove the lingering grief. "He heals the brokenhearted and binds up their wounds" (Psalm 147:3).

Remember, I am with you in your sorrow and long to bring you comfort and peace. Let me take your burden of grief and replace it with the joy of the memories you shared with your pet. "Come to me, all you who are weary and burdened, and I will give you rest" (Matthew 11:28).

Your pet's love and presence in your life were part of my plan to show you the beauty of my creation and the depth of my love. As you reflect on your time together, let those memories bring a smile and warmth to your heart. It is time to let go of the sorrow and embrace the healing I offer.

Know that I am here for you, always ready to listen and comfort you. You are never alone in your pain; my love for you is unending. Trust in me to guide you through this season of healing and to fill your heart with peace and joy.

With all My love,

Your King of Kings

Who do you need to forgive? Write your prayer about your pet to me. If your pet needs my healing touch, write your prayer here.

_____

_____

_____

_____

CHAPTER FIFTEEN

I KNOW YOU'RE GRIEVING

Dear Apple of My eye, I see the pain and sorrow you are carrying from losing your loved one. When someone accepts me into their heart, and they pass away, know they are in heaven with me. When a baby or child passes away, they are also in heaven with me.

It's okay to feel angry, even at me, for thinking I took them too soon. Come to me in your sadness and anger and tell me how you feel. Please release all the grief, sorrow, guilt, and shame. You have been mourning for too long. There is a time when you grieve, but now it's time to give it to me. I want to release your heartache, grief, and despair. I want to remove your sadness in exchange for joy.

I know the deep pain, and I am here with you in your grief. The ache you feel is a testament to the love you shared and a natural part of your journey. Though the burden of loss feels heavy, remember that I am here to carry it with you. My love and support are not temporary, but everlasting. Lean on Me, and I will provide comfort and peace, lifting the weight from your heart. Your loved one is safe in My embrace, and I will guide you through this challenging time, surrounding you with My love and strength.

Allow yourself to laugh again. Allow yourself to smile and have fun again. Please take off the grave clothes; it's time to live. Live your life to the fullest. The enemy has kept you in bondage long enough. "The Spirit of the Lord is on me because he has anointed me to proclaim good news to the poor. He has sent me to proclaim freedom for the prisoners and recovery of sight for the blind, to set the oppressed free" (Luke 4:18). I am setting the captives free. My yoke is easy, and my burden is light.

My child, know I am always with you, even in your deepest sorrow. Let me comfort you and give you peace. "The Lord is close to the brokenhearted and saves those who are crushed in spirit" (Psalm 34:18). Embrace my love and let it heal your heart.

With Deepest Compassion,

Your Comforter and Father

Are you ready to release the grief and sorrow to me? Write me a prayer about how you are feeling and how I can comfort you today.

_____

_____

_____

_____

CHAPTER SIXTEEN

✝
👑

I LOVE MY CHURCH AND PASTORS

— · · ● · · —

Dear Faithful One, I see the hurt you've experienced from the church, and I want you to know that it wasn't me who caused this pain. Please forgive my sons and daughters who have hurt you. I will speak to them about it. I understand feelings of disappointment and rejection, and I want to bring healing to your heart today.

I am deeply sorry for the times you were hurt within my church. I know you looked up to your pastors as spiritual fathers, and feeling rejected by them has left a wound. But remember, I never rejected you. I love you with an everlasting love.

I am sorry your pastor wasn't emotionally available when you needed them and that you felt the church wasn't there for you. These experiences have hurt you deeply, and I want to heal those wounds. I don't want anything to come between us—not a church building, a pastor, or anyone else. Come closer to me, my child, and let me heal you.

Talk to me about your pain and disappointment. Let me carry these burdens for you. Will you forgive my people? I know it isn't easy, but forgiveness will open the door to your healing. The church is meant to be a place of worship and fellowship, and I am sorry that your experience has caused you to feel otherwise.

I want to guide you to a church where you can find the fellowship you need with other believers. Will you be open to going? There are people I want you to meet, relationships that will enrich your faith and support your journey. Trust me to lead you to the right place to reconnect and find a loving community. Are you willing to go if I lead you back to the same church?

You are part of the ecclesia, My called-out assembly, and together, you are the church, My living body on Earth. The church is meant to be a safe haven filled with love and support, where My presence and grace are felt. However, remember that the church is made up of imperfect humans, each with their own struggles. While it can sometimes fall short, know that I am with you, guiding you all. Show each other compassion, forgiveness, and understanding; together, you will build a community that reflects My love.

I long for you to experience the joy and support of being part of my body, the church. Let me heal your heart, and together, we can move forward. I am here, holding you with everlasting love, ready to mend what has been broken.

With all My love,

Your Lord of Lords

Are you ready to forgive? Write your forgiveness prayer to me here.

_____

_____

_____

_____

Let's Bless:

Father God, I come before You with a heart full of gratitude and love for my pastors. Thank You for Your leadership, dedication, and unwavering commitment to Your service. Today, I lift them in prayer, asking for Your abundant blessings and favor upon their lives.

I declare that my pastors are honored and respected. They are recognized for their hard work and dedication to Your kingdom. I bless my pastors and ask that You pour out Your blessings upon them, meeting every need and desire of their hearts.

Father, may my pastors be highly favored in all they do. Let them walk in righteousness and integrity, reflecting Your character in every aspect of their lives. Grant them a spirit of excellence so they do their best for Your glory.

I pray that my pastors walk in morality, upright principles, and character. Fill them with wisdom, knowledge, and understanding so that they may lead with perfect discernment. Increase their finances, and their faith and hope continue to grow stronger daily.

Strengthen my pastors, Lord, and anoint them for the work You have appointed them to do. Let them walk in miracles, signs, and wonders, demonstrating Your power and love to all they encounter. May the

Holy Spirit rest mightily upon them, filling them with love and compassion.

Grant my pastors heavenly dreams and visions, guiding them with Your divine insight. Surround them with guardian angels, protecting them from all harm. Let them hear Your voice clearly and not be swayed by the enemy.

May my pastors speak truth, walk in truth, and preach in truth and the love of Christ. Help them to be fair, just, and trustworthy in all their dealings. Let them be respected, esteemed, and celebrated by those they serve.

Lord, I pray that my pastors feel loved, appreciated, and valued. Let them always know how much they mean to our community and me. I love my pastors and their families, and I ask that You bless them abundantly in every area of their lives.

I pray Psalm 91 over them, asking for divine protection and the assurance that they dwell in the shelter of the Most High, under Your wings, safe and secure in Jesus' name. Amen.

I bless and honor you, My child, as YOU are a minister of the gospel:

Dear Friend,

You are a gospel minister, and I declare you are honored and respected. You are recognized for your hard work and dedication to my Kingdom by me. I see you, bless you, and pour out my blessings upon you, meeting every need and desire of your heart.

You are highly favored in all that you do. You walk in righteousness and integrity, reflecting my character in every aspect of your life. I gave you a spirit of excellence that you may always do your best for my glory.

You walk in morality, upright principles, and character. I fill you with wisdom, knowledge, and understanding so that you will lead with perfect discernment. Your finances are increasing, and your hope and faith are growing stronger daily.

I strengthen you and anoint you for the work I have appointed you to do. You will walk in miracles, signs, and wonders, demonstrating my power and love to all you encounter. The Holy Spirit rests mightily upon you, filling you with love and compassion.

You will have heavenly dreams and visions at a greater level, guiding you with my divine insight. I surround you with guardian angels, protecting you from all harm. You hear my voice clearly and are not swayed by the enemy. You speak truth, walk in truth, and preach in truth and the love of Christ. You are fair, just, and trustworthy in all your dealings.

You are respected, esteemed, and celebrated by those you serve. I, the Lord God, respect you, esteem you, and celebrate you. I approve you, and you do not need anyone else's approval. You are loved, appreciated, and valued. Always know how much you mean to me and your community. I love you and bless you and your family abundantly in every area of your lives.

I pray Psalm 91 over you, asking for divine protection so that you dwell in the shelter of the Most High, under my wings, safe and secure all the days of your life.

Love always,

Your best friend

CHAPTER SEVENTEEN

✝

I LOVE YOUR FRIENDS

— ··•·· —

My beloved child,

I see the deep love and concern you have for your friends. Your desire for them to be saved and forgiveness reflects my heart. I also want them to choose Christ and receive the same peace and comfort that you have found in Him.

You have had friends for a season, a reason, or a lifetime. Every person who comes into your life is not a coincidence. I place people in your path with purpose, and sometimes this tests your character, strengthens your faith, and gives you an opportunity to share my love and truth.

Each friend you have is a unique blessing. Some friends are there to support you during specific times of your life, while others may be with you through all seasons. Cherish each relationship and see it as an opportunity to reflect my love.

Pray for your friends. Bring their names before me and ask for their salvation. Pray they open their hearts to my love and grace, just as you have. Your prayers are powerful, and I hear each one. "Therefore I tell you, whatever you ask for in prayer, believe that you have received it, and it will be yours" (Mark 11:24).

Live as an example of my love and grace. Let your life be a testimony of my transforming power. Show your friends the peace and comfort that comes from knowing me. "In the same way, let your light shine before others, that they may see your good deeds and glorify your Father in heaven" (Matthew 5:16).

Be patient and trust in my timing. I work in their hearts, even if you cannot see it. Continue to love them, support them, and pray for them. "The Lord is not slow in keeping his promise, as some understand slowness. Instead, he is patient with you, not wanting anyone to perish, but everyone to come to repentance" (2 Peter 3:9).

Know that I am with you on this journey. I am guiding you and giving you the strength to be a light in your life. Trust in me and continue to walk in my love and truth.

With all My love,

Your Faithful Friend

Are you ready to forgive a friend? Write your forgiveness prayer to me here. Please tell me how I can help you.

CHAPTER EIGHTEEN

I LOVE YOUR MARRIAGE

My Precious,

I see the pain and hurt you have endured from your past relationship, and I want to bring you healing and peace. Come to me and forgive your ex-spouse. You don't have to agree with everything they did but come to me to forgive them so that you will be free. Forgiveness is for you.

Forgive what they did to you. Forgive the past hurts and pain. Forgive the agony that you felt. Forgive everything they did and how they treated you. Let it go and release it to me. Don't harbor hate for years; just let it go. Release it and give it to me. Forgive every past relationship or marriage and I can heal your heart.

Forgive every fight you had. I understand these conflicts have left deep wounds, but I am here to help you forgive and heal. I am deeply sorry for the abuse you endured. I am sorry they were abusive emotionally, physically, spiritually, or mentally. I am sorry you had to endure so much hurt and pain. I want to remove the trauma and heal your heart from the past. Are you ready to forgive your past?

I'm sorry they didn't know any better and didn't live up to their marriage vows. They were not equipped with the love and understanding that you needed. But now, I am calling you to release all that pain and let me carry it for you.

Forgiveness does not mean that you condone their actions. It means that you are choosing to free yourself from the chains of resentment and bitterness. "Bear with each other and forgive one another if any of you has a grievance against someone. Forgive as the Lord forgave you" (Colossians 3:13).

As you forgive, you will find that your heart becomes lighter and your spirit more joyful. Allow me to fill the spaces left by your pain with my love and peace. "And the peace of God, which transcends all understanding, will guard your hearts and your minds in Christ Jesus" (Philippians 4:7).

My child, I want you to live a life full of joy and freedom. Let go of the past and embrace what I have for you. Trust in my plan and my love for you. I am with you always, ready to support and guide you.

With all My love,

Papa God

Are you ready to forgive? Write your forgiveness prayer to me here. Tell me how I can help you.

_____

_____

_____

_____

CHAPTER NINETEEN

I LOVE THAT YOU WANT TO BE MARRIED

My Bride,

I see the longing of your heart to be married. During your singleness, I have been preparing you for this special union. There are some things in marriage that you may find challenging because you are used to your way of doing things. Marriage requires commitment, love, sacrifice, humility, strength, and unselfishness. It is not about giving 50 percent but rather giving 100 percent of yourself and your partner giving 100 percent.

I am getting you ready for marriage. Come to me with all of your concerns about marriage. I am healing your heart and making it ready for a relationship. You have been hiding, thinking you are not prepared. You have to be ready to be vulnerable and willing to be seen. Make room for the new.

I know you are scared, but I've got you. I am with you in this process. Marriage will bring joy, companionship, and shared purpose but will also require effort and dedication. Be open to learning and growing with your future spouse. Embrace the journey with patience and trust. "Love is patient, love is kind. It does not envy, it does not boast, it is not proud. It does not dishonor others, it is not self-seeking, it is not easily angered, it keeps no record of wrongs" (1 Corinthians 13:4-5).

As you prepare for this next chapter, let go of any fears or doubts. Trust in me and my timing. "Do not be anxious about anything, but in every situation, by prayer and petition, with thanksgiving, present your requests to God" (Philippians 4:6).

You are ready for this, my child. Embrace the vulnerability and openness that love requires. Know that I am with you every step of the way, guiding and supporting you. I am molding you into the person you need to be for your spouse and preparing them for you.

Make room for the new. Allow yourself to dream and hope for the beautiful future I have planned for you. "Trust in the Lord with all your heart and lean not on your own understanding; in all your ways submit to him, and he will make your paths straight" (Proverbs 3:5-6).

Remember, I am your Father, and I love you deeply. I want the best for you, and I am with you always.

With all My love,

Your Bridegroom

Write your prayer to me. Share your fears, ambitions, and concerns.

_____

_____

_____

_____

SECTION FOUR

LOVING OTHERS

CHAPTER TWENTY

I LOVE YOUR PERSONALITY

My Beloved Children,

I created each of you with unique personalities and strengths, reflecting My infinite wisdom and creativity. Your differences are beautiful and essential for creating a balanced and thriving family and workplace. Let Me share how these traits can be seen as the mouth, mind, hands, and feet of the workplace, along with their strengths and suitable job roles. The four personality types I refer to are Sanguine, Melancholic, Choleric, and Phlegmatic.

Sanguine: The Mouths of the Workplace

I crafted the sanguine individuals to be vibrant and enthusiastic communicators. Their natural charisma and sociability make them the voices that connect and inspire others. They excel in roles that require interaction, motivation, and relationship-building.

Strengths:

- ✓ Exceptional communication skills

- ✓ High energy and positivity

- ✓ Ability to build strong relationships and boost team morale

Job Titles:

- ✓ Sales Representative

- ✓ Customer Service Manager

- ✓ Public Relations Specialist

- ✓ Event Coordinator

Melancholic: The Minds of the Workplace

I designed melancholic individuals to be thoughtful and analytical thinkers. Their ability to delve deeply into details and approach problems precisely makes them the minds that bring clarity and order. They thrive in roles that require careful planning, research, and attention to detail.

Strengths:

Strong analytical and problem-solving skills

High level of accuracy and detail orientation

Ability to think deeply and provide insightful solutions

Job Titles:

- ✓ Data Analyst

- ✓ Research Scientist

- ✓ Accountant

- ✓ Quality Control Specialist

Choleric: The Hands of the Workplace

I created choleric individuals to be decisive and action-oriented leaders. Their drive and determination make them the hands that get things done, moving projects forward efficiently and confidently. They are well-suited for leadership, strategic planning, and goal achievement roles.

Strengths:

- Strong leadership and decision-making abilities

- High level of productivity and efficiency

- Ability to motivate and direct teams toward success

Job Titles:

- Project Manager

- Executive Director

- Entrepreneur

- Operations Manager

Phlegmatic: The Feet of the Workplace

I formed phlegmatic individuals to be calm and reliable supporters. Their steady and peaceful nature makes them the feet that provide stability and support, ensuring a harmonious work environment. They excel in roles that require patience, mediation, and consistent support.

Strengths:

- Strong ability to remain calm under pressure

- High level of reliability and dependability

- Ability to mediate and foster a collaborative environment

Job Titles:

- Human Resources Specialist

- Counselor

- Administrative Assistant

- Mediator

CHAPTER TWENTY-ONE

I LOVE SANGUINES

— · · ● · · —

Dear Sanguine Children,

I see the challenges you face in your workplace and your interactions with your coworkers. I am with you in every situation, offering guidance, strength, and wisdom to navigate these relationships with grace and integrity.

Remember to treat others with kindness and respect in your workplace, even when it is difficult. Reflect on My love in your actions and words, and be a light in your environment. When conflicts arise, seek to understand rather than to be understood. Listen with empathy and respond with compassion, for a gentle answer turns away wrath, but a harsh word stirs up anger.

Jesus taught you to love your neighbor as yourself. Apply this principle to your coworkers, showing patience, forgiveness, and humility. When you face unfairness or misunderstandings, bring your concerns to Me in prayer. Trust that I will give you the wisdom to respond appropriately and the courage to stand for what is right.

Maintain a spirit of excellence in all you do. Work diligently and with integrity, as if you are working for Me and not just for human approval. Your attitude and effort can be a powerful testimony of your faith and dedication.

When you feel overwhelmed or discouraged, come to Me for rest and renewal. Cast your anxieties on Me, for I care for you deeply. I am your source of peace, and My strength is made perfect in your weakness. Lean on Me, and I will provide the grace you need to endure and thrive.

Build healthy relationships with your coworkers by being trustworthy and supportive. Encourage one another and build each other up. Remember, you are part of a team, and your positive influence can make a significant difference.

If you face challenges with specific individuals, pray for them and ask Me to soften their hearts and guide your interactions. Seek reconciliation and harmony, but also establish healthy boundaries when necessary.

Above all, please keep your eyes on Me. Let your conduct reflect My love, truth, and trust that I am working through you to bring about good in your workplace. Your faithfulness in small things will be rewarded, and your light will shine brightly, drawing others to Me.

With everlasting love,

God

CHAPTER TWENTY-TWO

I LOVE MELANCHOLICS

Dear Melancholic Children,

I know the depths of your heart and mind. You are wonderfully and fearfully made, intricately designed with a purpose and a personality that reflects My thoughtful craftsmanship. Let's talk about the melancholic personality and its invaluable role in the workplace.

The melancholic personality is characterized by deep thinking, analytical precision, and a keen sense of detail. Your ability to see beyond the surface, understand complexities, and offer thoughtful insights is a gift from Me. In the workplace, you bring depth, structure, and a sense of meticulous care that is often unmatched.

Your attention to detail and commitment to excellence reflect my own nature. I created the universe with precision and care, and I delight in seeing these attributes mirrored in you. Your work ethic, reliability, and ability to produce high-quality work are crucial in creating an environment of trust and respect.

Understand that your thoughtful nature, while a strength, can sometimes lead to feelings of overwhelm or anxiety. When you feel the weight of expectations or the pressure to achieve perfection, know I am with you. Lean on Me for strength and peace. It is not perfection I seek but a willing and dedicated heart. Your best efforts, offered in love, are more than enough.

Your analytical mind and cautious approach can provide balance and perspective in the workplace. While others may rush ahead, your careful consideration ensures that decisions are well thought out and risks are minimized. Your ability to foresee potential challenges and to plan accordingly is a strength that brings stability and wisdom to your team.

Your sensitivity and empathy are also gifts that should not be underestimated. You can understand and support your colleagues on a deep level, offering a listening ear and a compassionate heart. This creates a workplace environment where people feel valued and understood, fostering unity and cooperation.

I encourage you to embrace your melancholic nature with confidence and grace. Use your strengths to bring excellence, depth, and compassion to your workplace. Your role is vital, and your contributions are significant. Feel free to share your insights and to lead with your unique perspective.

Remember, My beloved, that I am always with you, guiding and supporting you. Trust in My love and know that you are valued for who you are. Your personality is a beautiful reflection of My careful design, and I am proud of the person you are becoming.

With all My love and grace,

Your Gracious Leader

CHAPTER TWENTY-THREE

I LOVE CHOLERICS

Dear Choleric Children,

I see you, and I know the strength and determination that reside within you. You are uniquely crafted with a purpose and a personality that reflects My power and resolve. I'd like to talk to you about the choleric personality and its significant role in the workplace.

The choleric personality is marked by leadership, decisiveness, and an unyielding drive to achieve. You possess a natural ability to lead, to take charge of situations, and to inspire others with your vision and determination. These traits are gifts from Me, meant to guide, motivate, and bring about positive change.

Your presence in the workplace is a catalyst for progress. Your confidence and ability to make decisions quickly and effectively are essential in moving projects forward and achieving goals. Your colleagues look to you for direction and assurance, finding strength in your unwavering commitment to excellence.

Your drive to achieve and your focus on results reflect my purpose and determination. I have given you these abilities to bring about my plans and to lead others with integrity and wisdom. However, remember that with great power comes great responsibility. Your strength can be a source of inspiration but can also be overwhelming if not tempered with patience and empathy.

Seek My guidance in balancing your assertiveness with compassion. Listen to the perspectives of those around you and value their contributions. Your ability to lead is enhanced when you build up and empower others, creating a team that works together in harmony and unity.

When challenges arise, remember that I am with you. Lean on Me for wisdom and discernment. Trust in My guidance to help you navigate difficult decisions and complex situations. Your confidence is rooted in Me, and with Me by your side, you can overcome any obstacle.

Embrace your choleric nature with humility and grace. Use your strengths to lead with integrity, inspire with vision, and achieve purposefully. Your role in the workplace is vital, and your influence is far-reaching. Feel free to step into the leadership roles I have prepared for you, knowing I am equipping you for every task.

Remember, My beloved, that I am always with you, guiding and supporting you. Trust in My love and know that you are valued for who you are. Your personality is a powerful reflection of My strength and determination, and I am proud of the person you are becoming.

With all My love and guidance,

Immanuel

CHAPTER TWENTY-FOUR

I LOVE PHLEGMATICS

Dear Phlegmatic Children,

I know the peace and steadiness that dwell within you. You are wonderfully created with a purpose and a personality that reflects My wisdom and tranquility. Today, I want to speak to you about the phlegmatic personality and its essential role in the workplace.

The phlegmatic personality is marked by calmness, reliability, and a gentle spirit. You bring peace and stability to those around you, creating an environment where others feel safe and supported. Your presence is like a calming breeze, bringing balance and harmony to the workplace.

Your ability to remain composed under pressure, to listen with empathy, and to approach situations with patience and understanding are gifts from Me. These qualities are vital in creating a workplace where people feel valued and respected. Your steady demeanor helps to diffuse tension and foster a collaborative atmosphere.

Your reliability and consistency reflect my faithfulness. I delight in seeing these attributes reflected in you. Your colleagues depend on you, knowing you will follow through on your commitments and provide support when needed. Your quiet strength is a foundation upon which others can build.

Understand that your desire for harmony, while a strength, can sometimes lead to avoidance of conflict or difficulty in asserting your own needs. When you need to withdraw or hesitate to speak up, know I am with you. Lean on Me for courage and wisdom. Your voice and perspective are important, and I have equipped you to contribute meaningfully to every situation.

In the workplace, your phlegmatic nature provides a much-needed balance. While others may be driven by urgency or intensity, your calm approach ensures that decisions are made thoughtfully and that people are treated with kindness and respect. Your ability to mediate and bring people together is a strength that promotes unity and cooperation.

Your compassion and understanding are also gifts that should not be underestimated. You can offer a listening ear and a comforting presence, creating a workplace where people feel heard and valued. This fosters community and belonging, which is essential for a healthy and productive environment.

I encourage you to embrace your phlegmatic nature with confidence and grace. Use your strengths to bring peace, stability, and compassion to your workplace. Your role is vital, and your contributions are significant.

Remember, My beloved, that I am always with you, guiding and supporting you. Trust in My love and know that you are valued for who you are. Your personality is a beautiful reflection of My peace and wisdom, and I am proud of the person you are becoming.

With all My love and wisdom,

Your Wise Redeemer

Let's Pray:

Heavenly Father,

I come before You with a humble heart, seeking Your forgiveness for the times I have experienced conflict in the workplace due to my lack of understanding of different personalities. I am grateful for the light You have shed on this topic, revealing the beauty and uniqueness in each person You have created.

Lord, I ask for Your wisdom and discernment in my daily work. Help me navigate every situation with grace and understanding. Grant me the insight to recognize the strengths and value in each of my coworkers, even when their personalities differ from mine. Fill me with Your peace so that I may approach every interaction with calmness and patience.

Please give me the grace to extend patience and kindness to all my coworkers and everyone I encounter throughout my day. Help me to be a reflection of Your love and compassion in all my dealings. Let me be a source of encouragement and support, fostering a spirit of unity and cooperation.

I pray for a workplace culture that honors and respects one another. May we all work together in harmony, valuing each person's contributions and treating each other with dignity and respect. Let our workplace be a testament to Your love and grace, shining brightly for all to see in Jesus' name. Amen.

CONCLUSION

I have been reintroduced throughout these pages to the Heavenly Father, Jesus, and the Holy Spirit. I have felt the power of His presence, the assurance of His love, and the reminder that I am never alone no matter the battles I face. God heals the brokenhearted and binds up my wounds, renewing my strength and guiding me toward a future filled with hope and purpose.

I have learned that God cares about every detail of my life and sees everything. He was with me even when I didn't realize it. I have again forgiven God, myself, family members, and co-workers. Understanding different personalities has given me a clearer perspective on my family and those I work with. I choose to walk my journey forgiving and blessing others. As I move forward with renewed strength, I am encouraged and refreshed, pursuing my dreams with renewed faith and a commitment to bringing His kingdom to earth.

Forgiveness is ongoing. I will keep asking seeking, and knocking, knowing the door will be opened: "Ask and it will be given to you; seek and you will find; knock and the door will be opened" (Matthew 7:7-8).

His love for me is unconditional. The best is yet to come, and with God by my side, there is no limit to what I can achieve.

ABOUT THE AUTHOR

Chris is the founder of the International Marketplace Intercessor Association and Manager at Shift Global Operations, a business supporting wise men/women in the Marketplace through daily prayer. Prayer is a passion, and she believes in using it as a weapon in all life situations. She is the author of Marketplace Prayers: A Call to Transform Our World.

www.ingramcontent.com/pod-product-compliance
Lightning Source LLC
Chambersburg PA
CBHW070522030426

42337CB00016B/2071